DEAR

MOUNTAIN

A Poetry Collection

on Love and Loss

JOY JING

First edition August 2022
Published and printed in the United States of America
Library of Congress Control Number: 2022914290

ISBN 979-8-218-04894-5 (paperback)

www.joyjingdesign.com

TO MY LOVE

NOTE FROM THE AUTHOR

Dear Reader,

Through this poetry collection, I am inviting you into a window of my life. These poems were written to a beloved during the time we were together and to myself afterwards. The lines arrived as unexpectedly as the relationship did.

We first met on the ballroom dance team. He is named after a mountain. The poems are numbered chronologically from our first date, with a half number representing a second entry on the same day. You are reading a partial selection from the entire set.

When you come across the word "elf" in the text, it refers to a role I held at my alma mater, where residential Houses employ recent alumni to bake for events while living on-campus. The elf suite is downstairs from the House Deans' residence, and we would regularly prepare food in the House Deans' kitchen for student gatherings.

As a writer, I strive to stay true to unfiltered feelings and thoughts. It is my hope that you find moments of resonance, joy, and solace within these pages.

With Love,
Joy

CHAPTERS

FALL .... Page 11

O	Reflection
1	Letter to Parents (Part 1)
2	Emptiness
3	Love Nest (Part 1)
4	Midlife Crisis
4.5	Weakness
5	Heartbeat
6	Prelude
7	Jesse (Part 1)
8	All of Me
9	Teddy
10	Smiley
11	Gap (Part 1)
12	Inertia
13	Touch
14	Love Nest (Part 2)
14.5	Rehearsal
15	Jessi
15.5	Crisis
16	Penelope
17	Bruting
18	Bypass
19	Maintain
19.5	Meatatarian

20   Abi

21   State

21.5   Subscription

23   Embrace

24   Clothed

24.5   Commitment

26   Woodberry

27   Persephone

27.5   Muse (Part 1)

28   Starry Night

29   Love Nest (Part 3)

30   Opposites

30.5   Happy

31   Her

32   Visiting

33   Missed Call

34   Love Nest (Part 4)

35   Blessings (Part 1)

36   Impending

WINTER .... Page 57

36.5   Of Elves and Man

37   Letter to Parents (Part 2)

37.5   Sustenance

38   Death of a Life

38.5   Risk

40   Exhaustion

41   Future

42   Sunglasses

43   Delirium

44   Upgrade

44.5   Joint Evolution

46   Longest Night

47   Down Payment

48   Mountain and River

49   Christmas Eve

50   Green Text Bubbles

51   Retooling

52   Object Permanence

53   Mother Tongue

54   Amtrak

55   ER

56   NYE

58   Blessings (Part 2)

59   Wellerman

61   Growth

61.5   Breakup

SPRING .... Page 95

62   Mt. Right

63   Jesse (Part 2)

63.5 Gap (Part 2)

64   Redo

65   Gifts

66   Figurine

66.5 Loss

67   Space

70   Love Nest (Part 5)

72   Passing Love

72.5 Lost Members

73   Kintsugi (Part 1)

75   Greetings

76   Jarrod

78   Receipts

80   Kidney

81   Albanian Honey

89   For the Ages

93   Distance

104   Profile Photo

109   Picky

110   Loop

111   Parallel

116   Sepia

129   Michal and Mel

142   Well-Loved

153   Ambivert

159   Muse (Part 2)

160   Immortals

172   Reliving

187   Red Scarf Woman

200   Kintsugi (Part 2)

GRATITUDE .... Page 137

ABOUT THE AUTHOR .... Page 139

FALL

O
Reflection

Watching my reflection
Halfway across the bridge
I asked her
Who is he
To hold that much of me

1
Letter to Parents (Part 1)

I found love
In his touch

Well-read and social
Athletic, creative, and gentle
He is the most interesting person
I have ever met

He breaks all my rules
Yet still is everything I could ask for
I have no logical case to bring forth
Only an immense adoration

He is: my mountain of happiness

看来我不是一个孝顺的女儿。
但这是我真心爱的一个人，
就请原谅我这一次吧。

2
Emptiness

A new shade of loneliness has set in
Coloring the space which was once your embrace:
Safety, warmth, love
To be wanted by the one I want
What I wouldn't give to be in your arms
Again

3
Love Nest (Part I)

Birds gather leaves and twigs
To build a love nest
I cleared out a drawer yesterday
Wiped dust off the shelves
Polished the sink
So that you may feel my welcome
Written in every corner

4
Midlife Crisis

My parents are having a midlife crisis
They're picking up properties without a second thought
You sigh
I imagine unused tennis courts on expansive grass
A neighborhood scattered with magnificent mansions

We lived through all socioeconomic classes
My childhood was a blur
You reflect
I picture the six of you in a one-bedroom NYC apartment
Your formative elementary school years on a scholarship

How interesting
I note
My parents had their own midlife crises
When they abandoned coveted status overseas
To begin again in the ripe age of their forties

We've both progressed
From cramped quarters to comfortable homes
But my family chose
To relinquish contentment and start anew

4.5
Weakness

This weakness of mine
Falling in love so quickly and deeply—

Why, I envy that
A friend cuts in before I could explain
Some days I wish I didn't have the capacity to love at all

For my thoughts chase helplessly after his image
My heart swells with every touch
My yearning for love shuts out all other desires
And pain cuts deep in the absence of his figure

But I grin and say:
No, it keeps me from taking over the world

5
Heartbeat

Your arms envelope my body as
I lay next to you, taking in
Your chirping breaths
Your pounding heartbeats
And wondering
If the pulsing rhythms
Are yours or mine

6
Prelude

What do you want?
I finally mustered the courage to ask
Faint as a whisper
Our bodies entwined and breathless
In the gray morning light

Breaking the impasse you
Reached under my cami
My arms and chest elevating
Off they went: shirts, panties, briefs, ambiguity
And there we were

7

Jesse (Part I)

Two Jesses in my life
A good day if I speak with one
Today I talked to both!

Jesse's cousin-in-law once advised:
Closure never comes from the person who is leaving
Jesse tells me about his friends who sleep in separate rooms
Because, not in spite, of love

Jesse sympathized with dashed imaginaries
The perils of planning and caring more
Jesse and I raked over present quandaries
And how to take time to explore

The Jesses in my life are thoughtful and kind
At times, they also can read my mind
One day I shall bring my partner in crime
And ask: should this one be mine?

8
All of Me

Haven't heard from you
The void haunts with voices of insecurity
Have I come on too strong
Have I asked for too much

I walk to Silvia's
She proclaims:
If you scare him off by being yourself then
Good riddance

So I pray that one day
I could be all of me
Without hesitation or apology

9
Teddy

Someday I'd like you to meet Teddy
Perhaps on a road trip we'd take
Or to his wedding as a date
Today I consulted his empathetic wisdom

Have a rich and full life outside of him
See how he treats you
Find out what he's like when he gets mad
Move slow

Slow
Is the pace you walk
Not my march to the store when you became ill

Slow
Is the way you talk
Not my fall once I started to get to know you

Teddy, I'm afraid I don't know how to move slow

10
Smiley

Your signature emoji
Arriving late in the night
Informing me
Of your visit to my site

Is it innocent or naive
Flattering or disheartening
That it's been ten days
Before you looked up who I am?

II
Gap (Part I)

Awoken
I wondered if you'd want
A wife at twenty-five
A kid before thirty
I wouldn't
Who am I to ask that of you

12
Inertia

Newton's first law
Might as well be about love

A myriad of choices
Some conventionally charming
Others easy to confide
All of them more familiar
And yet
I couldn't help but continue
Careening carelessly toward you

You are a multifaceted mystery
Guess I have a penchant for challenges

13
Touch

When I caress you
I draw maps of love on each
Inch of your body

14
Love Nest (Part 2)

I bought new sheets
A proper pillow

You hearted my text
And I glowed

I thought this would be the day
You made my love nest yours

But then you went home with
Someone else

14.5
Rehearsal

Do you ever rehearse what you're about to say?
A question that leads to love according to the *NYT*
I used to think, "only for work"
But now I find myself rehearsing
Over and over
What I would say to you
And even then
I get nervous my words won't come out right

15
Jessi

Jessi flew in from the west coast
Her words weave wise tapestry
Adorning these bare dorm walls

The risks you are taking
Are more reasons to talk
Frustrations you hold now
Will only grow over time

What is truly good
Will come back to you
Many guys would be happy
To meet you where you are at

Your time is so valuable

15.5
Crisis

A hug
A car ride worth of updates with Dad
Two hotpots
Mom home from work at last
Serene neighborhood
Restful train ride
Anxious heart
Playing the part

Crisis is:
Trying not to enjoy this reunion too much—
This will all disappear if they learn who you are
Crisis is:
Trying not to miss their laughter and quibbles—
Banter won't be the tone when I bring home the one I love

It occurred to me then
Disappointment isn't rooted in fear
But stems from love and grief
Deep love and respect for my two unwavering supporters
Anticipated grief and guilt for their inevitable hurt

16
Penelope

When we dissected *The Odyssey*
My teacher marveled at Penelope's trade-off:
Welcoming home the beloved hero
And turning away bountiful suitors

I found it strange
To consider it a trade-off at all
For what could be better
Than to be in the arms of love
Free of unwanted advances and obligations

Then I met you
I suppose you and Penelope
Would have something to talk about

17
Bruting

The hardest naturally occurring substance
Can only be cut by itself
As diamonds spin and grind
Polishing each other

Sea glass, on the other hand
Tumbles and weathers in the vast ocean
For years to come
Before reaching shores rounded and frosted

Will we shape each other into brilliant gems
Or etch permanent scars on our facets?
Will we adventure like sea glass
Collecting stories of a journey
In each clouded speckle?

18
Bypass

It was past 1 a.m.
When I climbed into bed
Thoughts of you lingering in the empty space above
The moment I plopped my phone onto the nightstand
It rang
The chosen tone
Triumphing over Do Not Disturb
Heart racing
I reached over
Wondering
What I would've missed
If I hadn't given you emergency bypass
To my heart?

19
Maintain

Things last forever in our house
That pair of sharp scissors you borrowed?
It's old enough to vote
This stainless steel pot that bears soups and stews?
It's been here before me
Those red prom dresses
They're from bargain shopping in seventh grade
So too is this silver-plated jewelry
Picked up at a time we found a whole new world in
American stores

This is how we maintain things
My parents are methodical
What we take care of will outlive us
My parents are proud
They've taught me how
To shine dishes to sparkle in any light
To hand tumble linens and clothes
To labor over vegetables and flower gardens
To be gentle guests of our house

We've still got a small library from their school days
Marked lines and dog-eared pages
Immaculate cover and spine
I'd like to think this is how
They've taken care of their marriage

Not just grand gestures and bombastic speech
But intentional care in each detail of every day
Their love has withstood change and loss
And it will linger long after they're gone

19.5
Meatatarian

Why, are you a meatatarian?
You peered curiously at my plate
No, I eat anything and everything
Omnivore

Oh, that's not a dealbreaker
Chimed my friends
Meals will just be a smaller part
Of your many shared experiences

But what they haven't accounted for
Are the traditions
We won't be partaking in

You won't get to taste Mom's legendary red braised pork
A recipe she's adapted and perfected
Or try my centerpiece chicken alfredo party ring
The one I whip up for any gathering
Or share a beef hotpot with Dad
He'd prep for hours ahead of guests' arrival

I will order dishes you can sample when we dine out
But it's so much more than that

20
Abi

If there are olfactory time capsules
Abi's house is one of them
I visit less frequently these days
When I step through the front door
Its scent takes me back every time

I love my family but I don't like them
Abi mused for a moment
Grandma is the only exception
So we are going on vacation together

Love and like
Similar yet not alike

Abi, one day when you meet your better half
Who can be there when grandma cannot
I hope you will exclaim with joy:
I like AND love this person!

21
State

That time I left home alone
In tears intending to never return
I made my room stately
Pristine
No hints of a guest through the winter

This time I packed in a hurry
As the three of us drove out in the morning
The bed unmade
Trash bin full
Clothes dangling on the rack to be worn again

I am intrigued by this inverse relationship
Is there joy in the mess
As it reminds you of me?

21.5
Subscription

The ride back to Boston is never dull
Stories, debates, showcase of new music taste

I was nervous putting on your playlist
Skipping tracks and gauging the audience
Buy Premium?
It asked
As I ran out of skips

I hate subscription services
I remember telling you
Then I realized how
Love is a subscription service
I have unwittingly signed up for

23
Embrace

My favorite part
About sleeping next to you
Is
You reaching over
Embracing me in your slumber

24
Clothed

I got feedback from a roommate
Knocking on my door
It's scandalous, she says
To walk around in your underwear
I think your body is perfect
Though not all could appreciate
Even my robe won't do
So let's get you clothed too

24.5
Commitment

Who could forget that viral tour guide
Who fended off swarming crocodiles
The same way he scared away his ex:
I LOVE YOU! I WANT A COMMITMENT!!

No ravenous reptiles in my path
No rapt audience to entertain
I still want to scream into your face:
IT'S BEEN FOUR WEEKS! ARE YOU IN LOVE YET!!

26
Woodberry

Go to the Woodberry Room
She beckoned
Browse for poets
Alive or dead
Off I went
In the comfy chairs I read two
Then I borrowed four more
Inspirations I did find
With love poems on my mind
Upon returning home
I promptly passed out
Entering a fever dream of
Shifting matrix of boxes
An escape game of three interlocking floors
We were stuck in the middle
Until I figured out
How to align the half-moon symbols
Our passage no longer in doubt
It was past midnight when I woke up
Panting
Is this poetry at work?

27
Persephone

I find it odd
That the goddess of spring
Fell for the keeper of the underworld
One bestows life
The other bequeaths death

There's a Chinese idiom of sticking a rose on cow dung
When something beautiful is wasted
I wonder if that's how Dad may think of it
Persephone's arrangement
My love affair

27.5
Muse (Part 1)

When Dad courted Mom
He wrote her a letter a day
Mom made eager trips to the post office
Beaming with joy
Stashing away the notes in her drawer

As genetics would dictate
I too am a hopeful romantic
Believing
Someday I will meet the one
Who inspires me to write every day

Now that I've met you
My emotions and words flow endlessly
For I too
Have found my muse

28
Starry Night

I should've known that a bookstore café
Makes the perfect getaway
Your arm around my shoulders
As we browsed the selections
To your witty remarks
Before sitting down
Three egg dishes
You devoured
We walked among holiday light-strung trees
Passing by a proposal set of candles and roses
I brought you to my favorite esplanade walk
As you shared earbuds for an audiobook
We sat cuddling on the M2
I gave you a back massage too
I was hoping that you'd bring me to the formal
But this was so, so much more

29
Love Nest (Part 3)

I should wash the sheets
Rose-colored one hundred percent sateen cotton
The first bedding item I've splurged on
Now embedded with your scent

And wash your towel too
Four stripes matching mine
Now dotted with curly hair
Incomplete thought bubbles

Tomorrow
I note slipping into bed
Melting into traces of you

30
Opposites

You rarely go to the dining hall
I rarely eat out
You avoid sugar
I eat desserts first

I juggle two calendars
You keep everything in your head
I speak with unfiltered emotions
You observe quietly behind your glasses

But I know I loved you when. . .
You remembered my dance social
When setting our date
You wondered out loud about Persephone
When we walked past the pomegranate book cover
You donned full attire for the short trek between rooms
To be respectful to my suitemates
You reached over and tightly embraced me
While sound asleep

I tell you I find you fascinating
Being opposites
It is in these tender, unexpected moments
That I find myself in love

30.5
Happy

You're always so happy
You quip, caressing my cheek
What, should I add in some depression?
I wink
Be more angsty
You grin
What I didn't have the courage to tell you:
I am happy when I am with you
Do you feel that way too?

31
Her

You hypothesize:
If I were to one day disappear to another country
She'd be the first to realize I was gone
Why her? I ask
She's the most dependable and always picks up the phone
You reply
That's a bit insulting, I counter
Thinking how I never missed your unique ringtone
It's a compliment! You protest
Insulting to your audience
Who's my audience?
The person you're talking to, I bristle

All of the next day
I wondered about her
So I treated her to hot cocoa
At the place I asked you out
Sporting just-out-of-the-shower hair
In a similar ensemble as on our first date

This is how I got to know her
Your closest, most reliable female friend
This is where she imparted support for us
As she wished me the best of luck

32
Visiting

A month since our first date
Once again you hosted me
Extending love and assurance in your arms

As we compared holiday plans
I couldn't help but wonder
If I am just another entry
In your mental stack of to-do's
An additional appointment to memorize
In your list of people to see

I quietly slipped out to let you rest
You waved and said:
Thanks for visiting

You will head home soon
Will you have the chance to say to me then:
Thanks for visiting

33
Missed Call

One missed call
7:03 p.m.
My heart dropped
Outgoing call
Two seconds, 8:55 p.m.
My late reply went to voicemail
Outgoing call
Eleven seconds, 9:16 p.m.
A second try and you were out

Your missed call rings loudly in my mind
Does this make me less dependable
Less like her?
Would you still call me when you needed me the most?

34
Love Nest (Part 4)

What I thought was immovable
Hinges only on two shallow hooks
It's a wonder how physics works
Defying gravity with little support

David and I moved wall-mounted shelves
So that on this morning
You and I woke up together
On the right side of the bed

35
Blessings (Part I)

I am getting to know your friends
Remembering the names of your loved ones
But the only ones we
Could not be blessed by
Are those who wrote the rules
Ink chains
Suffocating
A forbidden love
Is my time now up?
Has my luck waned at last?
Tomorrow I will find out
And witness my heart burst

36
Impending

I hear we fear the thought of death
More than death itself
For death bears no fresh consequences
Upon the passed
Lights off
Curtains shut
But dread
Is carried by the living
While the show must go on

WINTER

36.5
Of Elves and Man

Misty drizzles outside
No longer conveniently cover
My state of mind
Volcanic
Tremors of cries
Persistent
Streams of tears
Darkening gray pillowcases
Stripping their silver sheen

Four faces on the screen
Not a single smile in sight
Are you doing alright?
She paused, not quite
No! I bust a grin
This is the eye of the hurricane
The storm will soon materialize

After she left, I realized
The House is not the enemy
But it succumbs to hierarchy
Ahead the steps are clear
I shall disappear
From those most dear

I thought I was to play George:

A murderer to be forged
But Lennie is already gone
And the question confounds:
Was that moment of relief
Not choosing whom to leave
Worth it, for me?

37
Letter to Parents (Part 2)

The one thing I dreaded more
Than being told to leave my role
Was how to deliver the news
I've lost the best home
You've seen me inhabit
I will shed the comfort of community
For strangers in a new abode

But the first question you asked
Was whether the potstickers were off
Because we labored over those
And you were afraid they weren't up to standard
No, no, they were fine
They were quite a hit
It's because—
A pause
As I rehearse the exact words—
I started seeing someone who
Still attends school here

Oh
Came Mom's reply
Well that's not so bad
Came a relieving conclusion
As you weighed my actions and the repercussions
Dad got mad at the school

Kicking off a political rant
Normally I would have talked back
But tonight I am just glad
That you are on my side
That you believe in being in love
And how I wish
That you will still be on my side
When you get to meet him in time

37.5
Sustenance

Usually when I'm exhausted
I gorge on food
Stocking up a sugar rush
To soldier on, to shuffle past
But in the last two days
My hunger has abated

You don't eat much
You noted at dinner
Digging into my nachos
Guess not when I'm sad
I shrugged

As if the tissues that hold up my body
Are now liabilities to be shed
Panicked living cells
Conspiring to surrender, to hide
As if to say:
Sustenance could no longer sustain
The substance of your pain

38
Death of a Life

I want to live one hundred lives
Before the end of my time
Some lives I choose to take on
Some lives gently pass by
This is the end of a life
To being an elf, I say a fond goodbye
But did this need to end
So soon, so rushed?
Do lives reincarnate?

38.5
Risk

I judge people on the risks they take
You said on our stroll at Middlesex Fells
Where do you place me on that spectrum?
You gave it a moment of thought:
Somewhere in the middle

Would you still say that now
When you are the risk I took
And I've come to face the consequences

40
Exhaustion

Five days
Sixty listings
Twelve viewings
Ten new acquaintances
Two applications

I stopped tracking calories
Not that I didn't want to
I simply forgot
And when I remembered
There were more pressing threats
To address

The conversation tonight
Around university politics and student affairs
Sounded strangely foreign
Have I stopped caring already?
Or am I retreating from the last entanglements of elf life?
Telling myself:
This wasn't meant to be
This isn't where I'm supposed to stay

Is this growing up?
Or is this grieving?

41
Future

Do you want my bed?
The possibility materializing
As I sat on your lumpy twin-sized standard issue
Yeah
Then you can stay over
A playful tap on my cheek
And I beamed at the thought
Of finally spending the night at yours

I've adjusted to your pace
Holding hands as we walk down the street
You say that now, but in six months you're gonna be like:
You walk so slow!
I laugh, amused
Secretly elated at the mention of six months

I dream about our future all the time
Am I finally hearing hints
That you are picturing it, too?

42
Sunglasses

My favorite pair of sunglasses
Came free from big tech swag
Yellow aviators sunny and large

The right side screw
Has never quite stayed put
The first time it ventured out
I panicked
For it was surely lost in the everything bag
After frantic digging
I felt its unique shape and sent it home

Since then I've taken extra notice
Each time
Fishing deep for the three-millimeter tool
Stubbornly cramming it into the shallow socket
Sliding the shades back into the cloth pocket
Today I thought I lost the screw for good
But once again
There it was

Is this some kind of metaphor for persistence
Installing my way upon the world
Or does it illustrate stupidity
Continuously repairing a piece of oddity
That could be replaced

But this one is my favorite
I protest against its track record
And I shall repair it for a long time to come

43
Delirium

Earth-toned rotunda
Fake plants on modern decor
I can no longer differentiate
Enemies and friends
Advice and vices

On our first date
You said you wanted to talk
But I did all the talking
Before you reached over
And finally kissed me

They say the loss of first love
Hurts the deepest
But this first grief
Hits like tidal waves
Intruding upon the shore of reason
Receding
Foaming
Demarcating its last visit

Let it flow but stand your ground
Eni says
She thinks you're mature for your age
But she wasn't there
When I almost dashed out of the restaurant crying

The act of holding back tears—
As you sat
Picking at gnocchi
Staying silent—
Is a labor of love

What made you think
A "live, laugh, love" sign
Would make me happy?
But the way you held me tightly, lovingly
In the backseat of our ride
Made me picture us like that forever
Made me wish you'd be more invested
In getting to know me too

44
Upgrade

Barely a month ago
I dropped off twin XL flat sheets
First deployed on dorm beds
Before gracing full mattresses in post-grad life

Weeks ago I was committing to
A double bed, dual occupancy
Soon at the new place
I will furnish a queen

My full bed and sheets
Now yours to keep
May they continue to embrace you
And our nights together too

44.5
Joint Evolution

I want a career but my wife may want
A husband home for dinner every night
Talking to the kids
Taking care of family
Niklas hypothesizes

When I'm forty I may want to focus on family
By then my partner may not be able to produce one
Then at sixty I may want another career but
My spouse may want to travel
Niklas shrugs

You see, I'll likely want different things at different times
And there may be partners more suited to each stage
Than to me as a person
Niklas explains
What a thought
That's assuming they don't want to grow with you
I suggest

I am baring my soul in these writings
Sharing with you
My needs, my fears, my hopes, my dreams
I think a relationship is a promise to grow together
And adapt to each other's evolutions
My love, do you believe in this promise?

46
Longest Night

You didn't let me send you off
When I offered to come along to the station
I asked:
Is this the last I'll see of you?
Yes, you said
I hoped you'd add: this month, this year
Then the car came and you disappeared

Long I paused at the keyboard
You had heard what I wanted to say
But this is a new day
Slowly I typed:
Have a smooth trip home. Love you
As I stayed behind, waiting
For your reply that never came

47
Down Payment

Parents arrived in town
In jovial moods unfit for an eviction
It is an expensive change, Dad notes
But every start of something new
Requires a down payment
The reason you got kicked out
I find inspiring!

My belongings packed in suitcases
Shuttled on longboard
Arriving at metal basement trapdoors
Glistening in December rain

Returning home
Mom spells out my name in her message
You made a good decision
Take it step by step
We are happy here

It's like watching a movie
When you know something the characters don't
And you are just waiting for them to find out
Says Lindsay, capturing my state
We exchanged tales of partners and families
Give and take
I don't recall what prompted her next line

But it was an enlightening moment
When she said
It's like tea leaves
You get out of it what you need

48
Mountain and River

You are the mountain
Immovable peak
I am the river
Coursing through your ledges, your veins
I descend from glaciers
My emotions pour out in
Voluptuous waterfalls
From your crevices, your cliffs

They say:
One can move a mountain
If one is determined enough
But I've chiseled art into your facades
Reshaped your terrains
I flood, I wane
I bring storms down on your windward side
Leave your leeward side dry
When I miss you at night

I kiss you at river bends
Nurture your crops
Nourish your animal friends
If that day comes
My last drop departs
And takes up residence in the ocean
May adventurers gaze upon you

Point to the place I've called home
And tell the story:
There was once a great river
Who graced this mountain

49
Christmas Eve

First dusting of snow
Sticking around
Just as I left town
Gifted kitchen sets
In a borrowed SUV
Sitting quietly in the street
Enthusiastic train conductors
Enthralled reader next seat
It's delivered!
Says a friend who purchased a desk for me
All done! They're inside
Says my future roommate helpfully
Angels do walk among us
How lucky I am
To be in their presence

50
Green Text Bubbles

Did you ever hear back?
Lindsay checks in
Nope
But I couldn't resist texting anyway
My speech bubbles colored lime green
Sent as Text Message
Notes the gray caption
I love you
She writes before takeoff
This guy doesn't deserve you

51
Retooling

People are only as needy as
Their unmet needs
Independence is rooted in
Secure dependence
The book, *Attached*, tells me
Anxious types feel there is something
Wrong with them

Does this mean I should revisit a prior poem?
That my longing is not a weakness
But a hidden strength for deciphering the world?

The first step
Amir and Rachel instruct
Is to fully acknowledge my need for
Intimacy, availability, security
And to believe they are legitimate

I've never thought that way before
My perceived neediness
And emotionality
Are legitimate

52
Object Permanence

I learned to ski
From my bestie
Who coached tirelessly
Morning to dusk
Now I'm recovering
In a hot bath
Readied by Mom
Who wished me luck

It's the second wave of grief
It's doubting object permanence
Angels in my life
I'm weary to say goodbye
If a life can be taken away so suddenly
What is lurking in that I
Cannot see
Cannot hear
Cannot touch

I'm reading Nikki Giovanni
Your soundtrack and the fan humming in the background
She writes:
Love never goes
There is only Transition

53
Mother Tongue

Dad's most jovial holiday
Arrived with his closest friends in town
All fluent in the mother tongue
A stand-up ensued
On a life story
Long overdue
Funny how
We learned something new
Required to sit through
And not dissolve
Into tempers unresolved
Hours retold, struggles and triumph
Of wisdom and lessons to count

Afterwards, I wondered what would've been lost
By not having access to the mother tongue
Was it admiration for the people I came from?
Or would pressure to conform compound?
Do close ties necessitate a backstory?
Or would they just add to existing worry?

I wonder if in your first meeting with Dad
You'd be interested in the stories he had
I too want to speak in your family's mother tongue
And be audience to the tales abound

54
Amtrak

I learned about
Luba the opera singer
From
Simon the injured junior hockey player
Turned
Fitness entrepreneur
His dad is seventy-six
His friend is picking him up
Last leg of an all-day journey
Our chats interwoven
Between sushi and spring rolls
Until my frantic texts to you
Our dancing partnership in doubt

I staked out by metal walls
Cold air gushing through the moving floor
As I held on to your voice
It was the first open communication
And I rejoiced at its conclusion
But I couldn't figure out
If I love you
And you said you love me
Then how did that moment
Hurt so much

55
ER

Right flank pain
I typed on appointment screen
We need to test your lung
Doctor Ida noted digitally
This morning I hurried to bloodwork
For a three-vial draw that didn't hurt
From a tech who was curt
In the afternoon I labored
Moving gifted furniture
Gadgets and blings
Amidst raindrops galore
Then came two emails, a missed call
How rare it is that I get voicemails at all!

D-DIMER HH
Declared the test result
An ER visit I was bestowed
Confusing entrance slot
Thorough check-in I got
Must I be parked on a stretcher
When I walked all the way here?

Lindsay once told me
She never met a doctor who walks slow
And mine bounces in her flow
Medical Gas Shut-Offs - Do Not Block

I'm reading the walls
More interesting than the clock
When a new nurse came
She brought four vials
An IV no less
Causing painful distress

CT scan after a while
Long I sat waiting for the verdict
Eavesdropping a comedic moment:
I don't have more info for you
But you're not gonna die right now
These vitals signs aren't of a twenty-five-year-old
But they're appropriate for someone your age
That's real, giggles a nurse under his breath
As I once again turn to the pages
That shortly came to an end

Another set of vitals
A harbinger for getting out
Says Dani the first nurse
CT scan returned normal
A change of personnel
Amelia the sonographer
Reassures nothing is amiss

It is almost 10 p.m.
Way past my ice-cream-for-dinner plan
As I munch on another block of

Emergency chocolate
In the most fitting occasion
EKG, no pain begot
All clear, says the doc
One last struggle, the IV is out

Although it has been a long day
I am joyous
To have shared the adventures with you
Over texts and voice messages
Reading your email
As I finished the book
Was the best welcome back gift
That I could've wished for

56
NYE

Does the earth know
It's getting older
Or does it dutifully orbit
Until the sun swallows it whole
Does the planet think
This occasion is special
When inhabitants swear to
Shed the past and start anew

Myself and grief, carrying
Love from friends
Care from parents
Trodding
Quiet brick streets
In well-loved boots
Lights on trees
Putting on the year's last show
In their warm twinkle glow

58
Blessings (Part 2)

Parents left town
After two days of settling down
Not before our long chat
About us, present, future, and past

How does someone adore his extended family
But not dream of having his own progeny?
He talked of parental responsibility
But not of his parenting proclivity?
Dad is particularly perplexed
Does he love you back?
Is he good to you?
Mom wants to know

More importantly, they chime
You don't need our blessings
We are your home base, your backup nest
But we are not guardians of your life, you know best
We don't stamp your marriage license
We can offer tips and lessons

Your decisions and love affairs
Your family and daily manners
Are yours to create along the way
Through all, we are here to support
But we cannot guarantee to have a rapport

With the person you love

Rest assured, if he comes to visit
We'll be polite and kind
But not necessarily a friend
For that, he'll have to prove
Through actions most of all
That he loves and respects you
That he's willing to sacrifice and reach compromises too
That he values your principles, ambitions, and dreams
And does not push you to conform with his ideals in vain

Yes, we are biased from personal experiences
One can't fully extricate from larger cultural influences
But if he is as independent as we are
Then you two still have the future you hoped
This is not the end of the rope
It's only been two months
A blip in the grand scope

Though you should weigh the parts of you forgone
If you choose to continue walking on
Do not underestimate your worth
Understand how he perceives you in what he puts forth
You can always come home if things dissolve
But we trust you to work through troubles and doubts

Love is persistence, patience, and practice
Love is putting the partnership first

The love you find will shapeshift and sway
It's up to you both to bridge differences
And keep conflicts at bay

That's it for now, we'll be on our way
Call us, if you have more to say
I watched as their car pulled away
Thinking
THIS is a new day

59
Wellerman

Wellerman came on
Teleporting me to that balmy night
We pranced, grooved, and hummed along
To your new favorite song
As we tried to track down
My roommate's van
This has been surprisingly unsuccessful!
You exclaimed after two loops around the block
It was after I returned to the suite
That I found out the plate was switched
We'd passed by the familiar vehicle
As spacious and tenacious as it is old
With a sticker that said:
"Mountains, please"

61
Growth

Five fingers on a hand
Each begins at varying ends
We don't lament their uneven lengths
For the unassuming thumb
Is often the most useful

I've told others
I'd be an elf for a while
The universe must have heard me
And made grander plans
Thus onward I march

61.5
Breakup

It was thirty minutes into two months
When you said:
I don't think this is going to work

Though our last call was devastating
I had hoped that my discussions with parents
Would calm some of your qualms
But the way you were late by an hour
Hinted otherwise

You knew something this time around
When last time
It took you a year to fall in love

You did say I have extremely rare qualities
Among them self-honesty
And being a fundamentally good person
In almost any sense of the word

But you were afraid our cultures would lead us astray
I would not make future kids eat in a certain way
You are a rolling stone with no definite plan
I am on a mission following a timeline
You didn't think we had much physical chemistry
That was the most hurtful thing you've ever said

I fell for the way you touched me
I caressed and held you
I asked for our first kiss
Touch was your second-to-last love language
But first of mine
Perhaps it was a lack of chemistry
Perhaps you wanted to plant some distance in your mind

Our first trip taken alongside friends
Was to Breakheart Reservation
I am down for some heartbreak
Came your joking text
Looking back I wonder
If that was some kind of omen
But the heart that is broken
Is mine

SPRING

62
Mt. Right

It takes time to find your Mt. Right
Mom messages
I know she meant Mr. Right
But this serendipitous misspelling
When she doesn't know your name
Helped me realize
Yes
You are a significant mountain in my life
But you are not
Mount Right

63
Jesse (Part 2)

Ah, rock versus water
Very Daoist
Jesse notes
When the water is calmest
It reflects the world
When the water moves
It obscures the view
But water always wins
Penetrating rock through persistence, in time

Everyone feels emotions
Whether or not they express them
It takes great energy to suppress feelings
Jesse muses
Your beloved thinks himself an
Unknowable enigma with
Different roles in distinct circles, who
Cannot reconcile an authentic self, who
Couldn't bear the risk of you seeing him whole

His perceived lack of physical chemistry
Is just a reflection of insecurity
Jesse notes
He has expectations not shared out of fear
Those gaps he projected onto you
For not having met his unspoken needs

I was once someone like that
Able to shift seamlessly from intimacy to work
At the cost of not being fully in either
Jesse reflects
Isn't that the definition of anxiety?
Thinking about all the things that are yet to come
While in the present

It is conversations like this
Four hours speaking candidly
Sharing observations
Debating reservations
Laying out unlabeled feelings
Collecting scattered thoughts
Over pesto pasta and poached eggs
Sampling sweet wine and dark chocolates
That I start to imagine
What a future could look like
With someone
Who relates and comprehends
Like my gay best friend

63.5
Gap (Part 2)

If you find someone who's older
He'd know what he's looking for
Dad suggested

David and I talked about it and we're going to get married!
Ronia exclaimed
He's six years older
So he has been ready for a while
Women tend to mature faster
You are doubly disadvantaged
Ronia sympathized

Youth is prized in the gay community
Jesse explained
Noting his partner being five years his senior—
The gap between you and I—
And more committed too

Does this mean I have to
Look for someone more experienced in this world
What if I want to grow with them
And not be beholden to their status or their views?

64
Redo

I love déjà vus
They are occasional visitors
But always welcome guests
I'd like to think that each possible choice
We could make in life
Opens up a portal like in *A Christmas Carol*
I'd like to imagine at the end of life
We have the chance to revisit and redo
A life with the fewest regrets
Déjà vu is just a moment of remembering
Having walked down this path before

My friends asked me:
Knowing what you know now
Would you have done anything differently?

Knowing I've lost a life
And that I've lost us too
I ponder each decision:
Becoming an elf
   Learning ballroom
      Meeting you
         Finding love
            Writing poetry
Because I truly, madly, deeply loved you
And that love produced art too

Yes, I would redo
Even if I'm in much ado

65
Gifts

Did you know that gift
Was my top love language
Before I met you
After you, it was touch

But I've gifted you
Gloves when your hands were cold
The book you'd wanted for a while
Snacks when you were sick
Twice last fall
Omelet takeout after you slept in
A full-sized bed for better nights
And the half-day I spent rearranging your room

In return
You never meant to gift the things I was left with
You sent new club recruits a budget and an address
Materializing in beauty mask and bath bomb
Alongside a half-hearted thank you note
From someone I didn't know
For contributions I didn't make
You left behind a yellow mechanical pencil
And chuckled that I could keep it
It was so
Replaceable

There is no photo of us to look back on
There is no keepsake I could hold
When I'm missing your presence

But the sticky notes I wrote that accompanied each gift
The card I presented to you with holiday presents
They were still on your desk
I wonder
When you'll put them to rest

66
Figurine

Single-haired brushes
That's how I painted these details
You explained as I examined your figurine
Here, this one's better
You swapped out the one I was holding
I am no stranger to painting
And I've used just the brush you're talking about

How I envy these tiny lifeless statues
Once held delicately in your hands
As you patiently positioned each stroke
Dipped in boundless affection but minuscule paint

In our next life
If we are to cross paths again
Would I rather be your painted figurine?

66.5
Loss

You have no idea
How much I want to see you
To hear you talk
To be held

But I couldn't tell
If that would bring closure
Or enhance the contrast in the
Gap of your figure
Silence of your voice
Absence of your scent

You left me
When I had already lost a part of myself

67
Space

I enjoyed modern apartments
Sleek and efficient
Then I found refuge in this aging townhouse
Once a stately New England mansion
Wide paneled wooden floors
Door knobs turning loose
Original keys you'd find in antique stores
Slowly I grew into the high ceilings
Felt at ease among French windows

Bedroom held me
As I slept, meditated, studied, ruminated
Living room cuddled me
As I read, stretched, created, hosted
Dining room entertained
Games, toasts, banter, introductions
Kitchen welcomed
Meals, drinks, laughter, desserts

Home is written in idiosyncratic quirks
Warmth is carved into the detailed ceiling trim
Love is polished into the sculpted marble fireplace

The way I can move freely and fill up the space
With thoughts and dreams
Is a luxury that I did not know

On our walk you said
You love the suburbs
Is it because
The large houses and spacious rooms
Offer you a place to dream?

70
Love Nest (Part 5)

All my life
I've wanted
to be wanted
And now that you no longer
Want me
I am off
To find a new nest
To rest

72
Passing Love

Violent delights have violent ends
Therefore love moderately
Lectures Friar Lawrence
As he marries Romeo and Juliet
Catalyzing six deaths

Sounds like you fell pretty quickly
You'll fall out of it fast too
It's a passing love
Reassures my mentor
Love at first sight with his wife

What is a passing love?

Is it driving on the left lane
Speeding by roadside views
Only to make a U-turn at the next light?
Is it igniting an Olympic torch
That must never be extinguished
Of hope in its warm amber glow?
Is it tossing a crumpled-up note
Across the classroom onto someone's desk
When no one is watching?
Is it the ridding of a kidney stone
As shock waves splinter mineral deposits
Into smaller pieces?

I've passed love
Passed past loves
Help me
Passing this love

72.5
Lost Members

My husband is at work today
Katherine explains
A Sunday?
Yes, he transports donor organs
Legally?
Ha, of course

Remember when
I joked you've got an organ in that toolbox
But it's not the one I want
This one, I tapped at your chest
Is
That's my favorite
You said

If I pass before my organs expire
And they come to collect my parts
Can someone tell them
I'm sorry, but her heart isn't here
She gifted it to a mountain
Never took it back
You may revive the tissue
It just no longer beats for you

73
Kintsugi (Part I)

Tell me
I will fall in love like this
Again
Tell me
This is not
The end
Hold my hand
As I pick up
Shards of this broken heart
And begin to make
Amends

75
Greetings

It is no longer
Hey Love
And I didn't want to
Write out your name like before
I typed and deleted
Hi
Hello
Left it empty
Then I went back and wrote
Hey—

76
Jarrod

She said I gave up too easily
And I did
I did
But the Jarrod I am
Is not the same person from
Five years ago
Neither is she
She brought spontaneity into my planner life
We did so many silly things together
Some I can't even speak of
Her husband is wonderful
They're now expecting a child
I feel so much happiness
For them to be in such a great place
But once in a while
When I come across her face
There's a glimmer of hope
And wonder
Of what might've been
If I were in his place

78
Receipts

You were in my life every day
Then you vanished without a trace
Were we a mirage?
Conjured in a rush
Dissipating just as fast

Marie Kondo taught me
To toss things that no longer spark joy
I've given away cherished clothes
Well-kept furniture
Prized plants

But these old receipts
I still keep tucked away
They hold snippets of us
Places we frequented
From our first date to our last

Why am I holding on
When their face value is gone?
The highs and lows
Of moments untold
In lieu of photos together
In absence of mutual gifts
These are the only physical mementos
Of our past

Thin strips of waxy paper
Fading ink and ballpoint scratch
Assuring me
You are not
A figment of my imagination
We went on—
As you called them—
Adventures

80
Kidney

Did you hear about that TikTok girl
Donating a kidney to her love
Who then cheated and departed
Making other exes saints by comparison

Who am I to complain
When the only things I've forgone
Are time, energy, money
Not a physical piece

I did not grant you life
And you will not take it away from me

81
Albanian Honey

How do you know it's love?
Eni asked
Pointing out my precocious judgment
It's a feeling
Passionate yet enduring
It's a willingness
To learn and put in the work
It's like tasting your
Albanian honey
Sampled from wild flowers on the highest mountains
Stunning on the first taste
Lingering long after it's gone

89
For the Ages

After a hundred poems
There are still thoughts unspoken
When I am awoken
Emotions unprocessed
Pouring out through tears
What I wouldn't give
To be in a perfect relationship
With you

93
Distance

They say
The farthest distance
Is being next to the one you pine for
Who doesn't know of your love
They also say
Distance makes the heart grow fonder

But what about the in between
When I am just a brisk walk away
Yet our shoulders never brushed
As we hurried along in a blur of anonymity

Perhaps it is what
Bessie once told me:
Heart is an elastic band
The more it is stretched by distance
The more it yearns to recoil

104
Profile Photo

Your face unexpectedly popped up
Mid-scroll
I froze
At your first appearance

You look
Exactly how
I remembered you
When we were last together
A month and a half ago

So this
Is how I'll recall your face
The warm tone
That sideway look
Barely a smile
Holding secrets and thoughts
I wonder if this is a new vision for yourself
Because this photo
Captures the you I've known well

109
Picky

Even when there are
Options galore
It is you
I want more

110
Loop

I am reminded once more
Why the saddest appear happiest
How the loneliest exude
Abundant warmth
It is more than
Empathy and humanity
It is a necessary belief
In receiving what is given

If I gift enough love
More than I could hold
If I spread enough kindness
More than I could muster
Would they return to me
Someday?

Does the winter storm and persistent chill
Bestow lusher blooms in the spring?

III
Parallel

Parallel lines are so sad
A classmate once said
They can never touch

We converged upon a fated fall
A sought-after opportunity
A chance encounter
Now as we maneuver
To stay out of each other's trajectory
Have we become parallels?

116
Sepia

Photographs can be aged fondly
With a splash of sepia
Old papers turn yellow
Powdered ink blurs
And we keep them in treasure chests

Your image glowed spectacularly
As I ran a fever
Recalling the night we cuddled
As you struggled with a mysterious ailment

When will this memory dissolve into sepia
When will I no longer wish
For you to be here
For you to be near

129
Michal and Mel

I adore social engagements
But when friends depart
So too the endorphin highs
In creeps withdrawal

Not today
After visiting Michal and Mel
And the fluffball that is Carnegie
We exchanged updates over charcuterie
Built train lines on the Scandinavian map
It was so familiar
Welcoming
That I departed feeling whole
It was an adrenaline rush
It was also. . . comfortable

142
Well-Loved

When an item is worn
Used
Served beyond its years
We call it
Well-loved
And we pass it on

153
Ambivert

It's been suggested to me
Extroverts
Like to switch things up
Introverts
Keep a few things forever
For ambiverts
Do we get both or neither?

159
Muse (Part 2)

I attended an artist's talk on disappearance
Her abstract colors in
Violent strokes across the canvas

Here I am
Painting and stitching an unfinished model
When my muse has long left his post

How do I know
When an unfinished work is
Finished?

160
Immortals

What the billionaires are trying to achieve
Investing in de-aging technologies
Is the same as daring explorers
Seeking the fountain of youth
Is the same as emperors
Sleeping among terracotta warriors
Is the same as philanthropists
Naming facades beyond headstones
Perhaps
Is the same
As my writing of this love
Keeping it alive long after we're gone

172
Reliving

Editing must be a form of time travel

Even after
Waves of passion have subsided
I still tear up at the molten love
That minted these very words

Even after
Agonizing pain has faded
I still shudder at the raw wounds
That carved out those lines

187
Red Scarf Woman

There is a film I watched years ago
Eni reminisces
A beautiful woman with a red scarf
Torn between two lovers

One, a burning flame of passion
Volatile, enthralling
The other, steady and patient
Ceaseless and whole
She chose the latter
I could not understand it back then
But now I am starting to
Eni smiles

I guess I'm with the younger you
I smile back
My best relationships last for two months
Still, I do not yearn for tranquil days
But those that arrive labeled:
Highly Flammable

I will know by the way
Our eyes meet
Our hands touch
Perhaps when I've grown older
I too will crave the calm

But for now
I shall dance with thunder

200
Kintsugi (Part 2)

An ordinary sheet of paper
Cannot be folded more than seven times
Leonard Cohen took comfort
In cracks that let the light shine through

How many times can a heart break
And still be rendered whole
How many times can my world fold
Only to once again behold

GRATITUDE

Art originates from muses and inspirations
From the past and from afar
To those whose love, whose wisdom, whose presence
I have leaned on, reflected upon, held close to my heart:
Thank you

To all the named and unnamed individuals
Who are much more than the stories retold
I am grateful for the light you have brought into my life
I will treasure those days you
Held me, repaired me, made me whole

To those whose encouragement I relied upon to publish
I hope this collection is everything you have envisioned
And more
This is the start of a life
I am honored to have shared it with you

ABOUT THE AUTHOR

Joy Jing is a dreamer, learner, and creator. Her mission is to live one hundred lives before death, and becoming an author is one such life—thank you for being a part of it.

Joy's professional background is in design, venture capital, and entrepreneurship. She is a community builder, visual artist, parody writer, longboarder, and web comic fan. Joy holds a bachelor's degree from Harvard, speaks fluent Mandarin, and practices power naps. She lives by the motto "life is uncertain, eat dessert first."

You may learn more about Joy and say hello at www.joyjingdesign.com

Dear Mountain is Joy's first published collection of poetry. There are more to come.

www.ingramcontent.com/pod-product-compliance
Lightning Source LLC
Chambersburg PA
CBHW031422120626
46545CB00006B/2228